QUESTA

Victor Bumbalo

BROADWAY PLAY PUBLISHING INC
224 E 62nd St, NY, NY 10065
www.broadwayplaypub.com
info@broadwayplaypub.com

QUESTA
© Copyright 2006 by Victor Bumbalo

First printing: July 2006
I S B N: 0-88145-280-7

Book design: Marie Donovan
Word processing: Microsoft Word
Typographic controls: Xerox Ventura Publisher 2.0 P E
Typeface: Palatino
Printed and bound in the U S A

QUESTA opened at The Court Theater in Los Angeles on 8 April 2005. David Milch was the Executive Producer; Joe Cacaci and Mireya Hepner were the Producers. The cast and creative contributors were:

SUSAN . . . . Alexandra Lydon
PAUL . . . . Michael Hagerty
NICHOLAS . . . . Tom O'Keefe
LORI . . . . Wendie Malick
FATHER JAMES . . . . Dan Lauria
DANIEL . . . . Dorian Harewood
RICHARD . . . . Bruce Nozick

alternate cast:

SUSAN . . . . Kincaid Walker
PAUL . . . . Adam Giordano
NICHOLAS . . . . Nick Hoffa
LORI . . . . Terry Davis
FATHER JAMES . . . . Bruce Nozick
DANIEL . . . . Harold Surratt
RICHARD . . . . Anthony Holiday

Director . . . . Joe Cacaci
Scenic design . . . . Evan Bartoletti
Lighting design . . . . Dan Weingarten
Sound design/original music . . . . Steve Goodie
Costume design . . . . Alex Jaeger
Casting . . . . Michael Donovan, C S A
P R/Marketing . . . . David Elzer/Demand P R
Stage manager . . . . Crystal Jackson
Assistant stage manager . . . . Morgan Lindsay Price

The author would like to thank all those involved in this project, and especially, David Milch.

CHARACTERS & SETTING

SUSAN, PAUL's sister, mid-twenties
PAUL, early thirties
NICHOLAS, SUSAN's husband, early thirties
LORI, mid-forties
FATHER JAMES, early forties
DANIEL, street person, mid-forties
RICHARD, LORI's boss, mid-forties

Place: New York City

Time: Today

for Eric and Michael

ACT ONE

Scene One

(SUSAN's *apartment. Evening)*

(A couple of set pieces indicate the living room of an Upper West Side apartment. It has a young, starting out feel to it.)

(The play has several locations. A couple of props and/or set pieces can define each location. The various environments should seem to flow into each other, creating a fluid feeling as characters move from one space to another. Each scene should easily turn into the next.)

(SUSAN, *mid-twenties, an in-shape woman, in leotards, is doing some stretching. She actually seems to be enjoying herself and her cooperative body.)*

SUSAN: One, two, three, four. Breathe, two, three, four.

(The doorbell rings.)

SUSAN: Release, two, three, four.

(The doorbell rings again.)

SUSAN: *(Irritated)* Damn, two, three, four. *(She goes to the door and opens it.)*

(PAUL, *her brother, stands before her. He is in his early thirties and wears a T-shirt, jeans, and baseball-type jacket. He is covered in blood.)*

SUSAN: Oh my God! What happened? Paul!?! What happened?

(PAUL *quickly enters the apartment. He is half out of his mind, hyper, and desperate. He starts ripping off his clothes. His speech is rapid and disjointed.*)

PAUL: *(Referring to his clothes)* We've got to get rid of these. Get me something to wear! No, I better shower first. Is Nicholas here?

SUSAN: No.

PAUL: When will he be back?

SUSAN: In a few minutes.

PAUL: I don't want him to see this. Get me a plastic bag.

(SUSAN *runs out of the room to get a plastic bag for his clothes.*)

PAUL: Then a drink. I need a drink!

SUSAN: *(Off-stage)* You shouldn't.

PAUL: I need one! Please!

(SUSAN *comes into the room with the plastic bag.* PAUL *grabs it out of her hands and starts throwing his bloodied clothes into it.*)

SUSAN: What the hell happened?

PAUL: The drink!

(PAUL *is now down to his underwear. He checks his body for blood.* SUSAN *goes to a cabinet and pours* PAUL *a drink.*)

PAUL: He's dead.

SUSAN: Who?!?

PAUL: I don't know who he is. But I'm sure he's dead. Oh, Jesus fucking Christ.

(PAUL *grabs the drink out of* SUSAN's *hand and gulps it.*)

SUSAN: Who is dead?

PAUL: The man in the alley. (*He pours himself another drink.*)

SUSAN: What alley?

PAUL: I didn't mean it. Not really. You believe me? Don't you? You believe me?

SUSAN: Paul, what are you talking about?

PAUL: I killed him.

SUSAN: What?!?

PAUL: I could have stopped. But I didn't. I kept hitting. Banging his head. It was that final hit. That's the one that did it.

(SUSAN, *in shock, is just staring at* PAUL.)

PAUL: (*Getting more hyper*) We were in the alley behind Trucking. It's a bar. Sex goes on in that alley. Don't look at me like that. It's the only kind of sex I can handle these days. No one was there but him. Younger than me. Bigger. He was drunk. Called me names. Then he started hitting me. Hard. Somehow I tripped him. There was blood coming from his head. He must have fallen on a rock or some glass. I jumped on him. Grabbed him by the shoulders and...I snapped. Kept banging his head to the ground until... Then I heard someone else coming toward us. And I ran. Oh, Jesus.

SUSAN: Maybe he's still alive.

PAUL: He's not.

SUSAN: You've got to call the police now.

PAUL: No!

SUSAN: You've got to! It was an accident. Self-defense. (*She goes over to the phone and picks it up.*)

PAUL: Put that down! They can trace the call!

SUSAN: Look, I'll come down to the police station with you.

PAUL: I don't want to go to the police.

SUSAN: Paul, you have to. Somebody could have seen you. I'm calling the police, and you're going to talk to them.

PAUL: Didn't you hear me? I kept banging his head. If you love me, you'll put down that phone.

(SUSAN *puts down the phone.*)

PAUL: I better shower. Could you get me something to wear?

(SUSAN *leaves the room.* PAUL *follows her.*)

PAUL: *(Off-stage)* What are we going to tell Nicholas?

SUSAN: *(Off-stage)* The truth.

PAUL: *(Off-stage)* No. Please, don't.

(SUSAN *comes back into the room. She heads for the phone and picks it up. She stares for a moment in the direction of the shower. She starts to cry. She puts down the phone.*)

(*The door opens, surprising* SUSAN. *It's her husband,* NICHOLAS. *He is a confident, athletic-looking young man.*)

NICHOLAS: One grocery store and two delis later...natural cashews. What's the matter?

SUSAN: *(Trying to recover)* Nothing.

NICHOLAS: You're crying.

(SUSAN *grabs the plastic bag that contains* PAUL's *clothes and leaves the room.*)

SUSAN: *(Off-stage)* It's my brother. He's in the shower.

(NICHOLAS *follows* SUSAN.)

NICHOLAS: *(Off-stage)* Why's he in our shower?

SUSAN: *(Off-stage)* He got here drunk. Got sick all over himself.

NICHOLAS: *(Off-stage)* I thought he stopped drinking.

(SUSAN comes back into the room with NICHOLAS following her.)

SUSAN: Well, I guess not.

NICHOLAS: We should have been more aggressive with him months ago. Done one of those interventions.

SUSAN: How many times do I have to tell you that wouldn't work with Paul?

NICHOLAS: *(Sarcastically)* Right, he's so special.

SUSAN: Please, leave him alone tonight. He's embarrassed. He's just going to want to go home.

NICHOLAS: Why do you keep indulging him?

SUSAN: He lost his lover.

NICHOLAS: Who was my best friend.

SUSAN: Sorry.

(PAUL comes into the room.)

NICHOLAS: Paul, this is serious.

PAUL: *(Shocked, to SUSAN)* You told him?!?

NICHOLAS: Of course she told me. You got here drunk and got sick all over yourself. This is a wake-up call, my friend. Give A A a chance, please.

PAUL: Tomorrow. I'll go. I'll go tomorrow. I promise.

NICHOLAS: Don't humor me.

PAUL: I'm not. Really. Tomorrow, I'll find a meeting and go. I have to sit down for a minute.

NICHOLAS: Let me make us some coffee.

PAUL: Hey guy, thanks. That would be great.

(PAUL *sits down. After a moment,* NICHOLAS *leaves the room.*)

PAUL: Thank you for not telling him. Nicholas hates me.

SUSAN: No, he doesn't.

PAUL: Don't you start hating me.

SUSAN: Never.

PAUL: He's lying there. In the alley. *(Suddenly bolting up)* He might still be alive. Maybe he's not dead. I've got to call 9-1-1. I'll call. I will. From a pay phone. *(He bolts from the apartment.)*

(End of scene)

Scene Two

*(*LORI's *kitchen)*

*(*LORI *is an attractive woman in her mid-forties. She looks tired and seems a bit drugged.* FATHER JAMES *is seated at the table. He is a little younger than* LORI *and exudes too much sexuality for a priest.)*

*(*LORI *wanders around the room aimlessly.)*

LORI: Father Dunn's eulogy was ridiculous. It had nothing of Will in it.

FATHER JAMES: I should have done it. I'm sorry.

LORI: And his idea of angels...

FATHER JAMES: Father Dunn's spirituality has a touch of Disney to it.

LORI: Why did God do this to me? Is it because of us?

FATHER JAMES: No.

LORI: How can you be so sure? I keep seeing my son everywhere.

FATHER JAMES: Does that bring you any comfort?

LORI: What the hell are you talking about? I want my son back. Not some ghost.

FATHER JAMES: Tell me what I can do for you.

LORI: How the hell did those people get my number?

FATHER JAMES: Your name was in the paper.

LORI: They called it another "gay" bashing. Well, I told them. They won't be calling here again. My son was not one of them. You know, I think some of the police think he was.

FATHER JAMES: No, they don't. The way his car was parked. He just ran back there to pee. Like the witness said.

LORI: He was normal, you know that. And how he would laugh whenever I made fun of Richard... Why the hell did he have to pee there? They better find out who killed him.

FATHER JAMES: They will.

LORI: Not if they think he was gay. His dirty clothes are still in the hamper.

FATHER JAMES: Do you want me to take care of them?

LORI: No.

FATHER JAMES: You have got to try to get some sleep.

LORI: Can you stay all night?

FATHER JAMES: You know I can't do that.

LORI: Your collar is very selective in what kind of comfort it can give.

FATHER JAMES: I'll stay for a while, though.

(LORI *leaves the kitchen.* FATHER JAMES *begins to undress. He makes the sign of the cross.*)

FATHER JAMES: Dear Jesus, please help her. Please give her strength.

(End of scene)

Scene Three

(A deserted street. Night)

(DANIEL, a black street person in his mid-forties, addresses the audience. He speaks in an elegant, slightly lethargic manner.)

DANIEL: I'm the witness. I saw it all. Heard it all too. I was peeing you see. In that alley. That place is a regular pissoir, isn't it? Impressed? I know some French. I heard what they were saying, and I heard the blows. The straight boy...I read his name was Will somebody. Anyway, "Will" said "faggot" with such contempt. Know that contempt. Felt it all my life. Felt it in a variety of so many names. Nigger. Queer. Faggot. Cocksucker. Coon. Fairy. Jungle bunny. Nignog. Fruit. Felt that contempt in all the beatings I've taken. I guess I was enjoying that fight. Seeing the "queer" beating the shit out of that boy. But by the time I finished up and started toward them...I was gonna yell or try to break it up...it was over. The gay guy heard me and ran. The straight boy was dead. I could tell. I've seen dead people on the streets before. It happened so fast. One minute so alive with all that arrogance of youth. And the next second...gone forever. I bet when they cleaned him up, he made one hell of a beautiful corpse. I did my civic duty. I walked into Trucking. Of course, they told me to get the hell out of there. I said somebody's been killed. That blew the wind out of their skirts. I don't know why, but I said there was a gay bashing. The term spread through the bar like fire. "Gay bashing...isn't it terrible...terrible." It is. Like all killing. It's terrible. The

cops were surprised I was so cooperative. I'm usually
not. But I thought, what the hell. I said, "For a cigarette,
I'll describe him. I'm easy." "Just for a cigarette, Daniel?
Why are we getting off so cheap?" "Because you're
seeing a kinder, gentler me. Plus you'll owe me one."
We all laughed. The cops sometimes pretend they're
friends with me. So I described him. He was over six
feet, blond, beefy kind of straight guy. Almost looked
like the victim's brother. (*This is the exact opposite of what*
PAUL *looks like.*) They brought in one of those artists.
You know, who try to draw what the person looks like.
I was with him two hours. Drank tons of free coffee.
Had a couple of doughnuts too. Said the nose was
wider. The eyes were further apart. Thin-lipped. The
artist was kind of cute. And it was raining out. So I gave
myself a civilized afternoon. Don't look at me like I'm
crazy. Oh yes, I've got "the disease." Had it for years
and years and years. It's not in my brain, if that's what
you're thinking. I'm a bit skinny, but I go on and on
and on. I know the "guy" didn't look anything like
the Hollywood hunk I described. Nothing. Well...
what began as a gay bashing...it had another ending.
I haven't slept well lately. If I hadn't been pissing,
maybe I would have gotten there sooner. Maybe not.
Keep wondering... How responsible am I? Am I a
murderer too?

(End of scene)

Scene Four

(PAUL's apartment. A few days later)

(Both PAUL *and his apartment look unkempt.* SUSAN *is
doing some straightening up.)*

PAUL: Why do you think he did it?

SUSAN: Who?

PAUL: The witness. The description he gave is nothing like me.

SUSAN: Maybe he didn't even see it. Maybe he wanted to get attention.

PAUL: I'm worried. He might know who I am. He might come to blackmail me.

SUSAN: We should have gone to the police...instead of sitting here and doing nothing.

PAUL: There is nothing we can do.

SUSAN: Then...we must never speak about this again.

PAUL: We won't be able to do that.

SUSAN: I'm sorry, Paul. It's the only way I can handle this.

PAUL: The mother...I hear she's a hairdresser here in the Village. I wonder what she's like.

SUSAN: Please. Stop it!

(Silence. PAUL goes over to SUSAN and touches her.)

PAUL: I never should have told you.

SUSAN: You had to. We've never kept secrets from each other. But... We have to cut what happened from our memory. Cut it out! That's what we have to do. We shared dreams before. Remember all those dreams we used to have after Mommy and Daddy died. They were always so similar. And when we would tell them to each other some of our loneliness would disappear, remember? Well, let's pretend...this time...we both had a similar nightmare. An awful one. We've talked about it. Now, we can forget it. Or at least pretend to. And we'll keep pretending.

(End of scene)

Scene Five

(RICHARD's *beauty salon*)

(RICHARD *is a well-put-together man in his mid-forties. Although shy and soft-spoken, he is a kind-hearted survivor.*)

(LORI *is in between customers.* RICHARD *brings her a cup of coffee.*)

RICHARD: How's it going?

LORI: Okay.

RICHARD: I went to the demonstration the other night.

LORI: It's ridiculous. My son was not gay. You know that.

RICHARD: But the killer thought he was.

LORI: Let's not talk about it.

RICHARD: You know, you can cut out early if you need to.

LORI: I don't need to. I just don't want to talk about Will.

RICHARD: *(Kindly)* I'll leave you alone.

LORI: I didn't say I wanted to be left alone, Richard. I just don't want to talk about my son. Talk doesn't help. It only fires up my pain. And I choke with it. When that happens, I don't want to be in a salon in the middle of Greenwich Village.

RICHARD: I understand.

LORI: Thank you. *(After a moment)* How have you been doing?

RICHARD: Worried about you.

LORI: Any dates this weekend?

RICHARD: I can't go there, Lori.

LORI: Distract me! We're supposed to be friends, aren't we?

RICHARD: We are.

LORI: Then distract me.

RICHARD: I'm going through a dry spell. This talk is absurd.

LORI: Please! Talk! Continue!

RICHARD: I went to a bar. The boys were so young. I was the oldest guy there. It's not just that you are invisible. They resent you for taking up space. I don't know what I should do. Any ideas?

(LORI *has not been paying attention to* RICHARD *for the last several moments.*)

LORI: There's my next customer.

(LORI *walks away from* RICHARD.)

(*End of scene*)

Scene Six

(*A deserted street. Night*)

(DANIEL *faces the audience.*)

DANIEL: You know, I've seen that gay boy, my little killer, before. Behind that bar. In the alley. He's the kind of man I've always been a sucker for. You know that quiet, polite type. He used to smile when he said "hello." I offered myself to him a couple of times. He said, "No, thank you." Real polite though. He's got a nice dick. Saw it once. He's kinda special. Now and then I give myself a treat, and I fantasize about him. I know where he lives. I followed him home one

night. He didn't see me. I'm not a stalker or anything.
I follow a lot of the boys home. It's curiosity really.
I want to know something about their lives away from
the alley. Don't know his name. But I'll find out. I bet
he thinks about that "Will," the dead boy, all the time.

(End of scene)

Scene Seven

(LORI's kitchen)

(LORI comes into the kitchen tying her robe.)

LORI: *(Calling into the other room)* Anything to drink?

FATHER JAMES: *(Off-stage)* A beer if you've got one.

(LORI gets a beer and places it on the table. FATHER JAMES comes into the room. He is getting dressed. They share the beer.)

LORI: How I wish you could stay the night.

FATHER JAMES: *(After a moment)* Have you been able to sleep?

LORI: Only a few hours a night. Maybe I should see a doctor. Get some pills.

FATHER JAMES: That wouldn't be a bad idea.

LORI: I called that detective today.

FATHER JAMES: And?

LORI: Nothing yet. *(Sarcastically)* But they're working on it. They're never going to find him. Do you feel guilty about our fucking?

FATHER JAMES: What brought that up?

LORI: I'm curious.

FATHER JAMES: Sometimes.

LORI: But not all the time?

FATHER JAMES: No.

LORI: I guess you don't take your vows too seriously.

FATHER JAMES: Some would say that I don't.

LORI: But you think you do?

FATHER JAMES: For the most part. Yes. You might not believe it, but I'm a good priest.

LORI: But by your own rules.

FATHER JAMES: That's what some would say.

LORI: I wonder where Will's father is.

FATHER JAMES: When was the last time you saw him?

LORI: Before Will was born. Do you think you can grieve for a child you never met?

FATHER JAMES: I wouldn't know.

LORI: I wonder. I broke a promise I made to you. I told Will about us. Don't worry, he's the only one I told. He had a good laugh.

FATHER JAMES: He thought it was funny?

LORI: In a way it is.

FATHER JAMES: Thank God, you didn't tell Richard.

LORI: *(Ignoring him)* I used to enjoy my work. Now, I hate it. Hate being around all those gay guys. It's like pity vomits out of them. I know what they're all thinking. "He probably was gay, and she just can't accept that." Such queer bullshit. I've started calling them names under my breath. I'm going to have to find another job.

FATHER JAMES: Maybe I can help you with that.

LORI: Just what I need. A church job.

FATHER JAMES: Lori, what do you want me to do?

(LORI *walks over to him.*)

LORI: Have sex with me again before you go. It's the only time I feel something other than this pain.

(End of scene)

Scene Eight

(SUSAN's *apartment. Some weeks later*)

(NICHOLAS *and* SUSAN *both seem to be glowing. A few presents have been opened. Ripped birthday paper is on the floor.*)

NICHOLAS: Did you like your gifts?

SUSAN: Yes, yes, yes.

NICHOLAS: Happy birthday. Are you ready?

SUSAN: I am so nervous.

NICHOLAS: Do you have the envelope?

SUSAN: Right here.

NICHOLAS: Did the doctor think we're crazy?

SUSAN: No.

NICHOLAS: Are you ready to find out?

SUSAN: *(Excitedly)* Yes. *(Handing him the envelope)* You open it.

NICHOLAS: *(Giving it back)* No, it should be you.

SUSAN: It's no longer going to be an it. It's going to be... Should I open it?

NICHOLAS: Yes!

SUSAN: Here goes. *(She opens the envelope. It contains the sonogram and a note.)* We're going to have a boy.

(NICHOLAS *embraces* SUSAN.)

NICHOLAS: *(Excitedly)* Oh my God. A son. Are you disappointed?

SUSAN: No. We can start thinking of names.

NICHOLAS: Not tonight. I don't want to label him yet. I just want to dream about him. But no family names. Something special and unique.

SUSAN: But nothing odd or trendy.

NICHOLAS: Or common. But a real name. Not Water, Breeze, Apple...

(SUSAN *kisses* NICHOLAS.)

SUSAN: Can't wait to tell Paul.

NICHOLAS: So you're finally ready to tell him. Well...we'll call him tomorrow.

SUSAN: He'll be over in a while.

NICHOLAS: You invited him?!?

SUSAN: Of course! It's my birthday. He's my brother.

NICHOLAS: But tonight is not a regular birthday.

SUSAN: He's my family. I want to share this night with him. After all, he's the only other person in my life that I love.

NICHOLAS: When I married you, I had no idea I was getting into a threesome.

SUSAN: Sure you did.

NICHOLAS: Too bad I'm not bisexual. At least I'd be getting more pleasure out of the situation. Can't tonight be just us?

SUSAN: It's mostly us. Be generous.

NICHOLAS: Why haven't you told Paul you're pregnant?

SUSAN: He's been too sad. I couldn't flaunt our joy in his face.

NICHOLAS: I'm beginning to think he works his grief. Any joy will always be buried in it.

SUSAN: Not true. And I'm going to pretend you didn't say that.

NICHOLAS: Sorry. But I miss the old Paul.

SUSAN: I miss it all. The Paul before Kevin's death. The world before the bomb. My childhood before having to live with my aunt...

NICHOLAS: All right, all right.

SUSAN: This city before 9/11. The Paul before the alley...

NICHOLAS: What alley?

SUSAN: *(After a moment)* We're going to have a son.

(End of scene)

Scene Nine

(RICHARD's Beauty Salon. Early evening)

(LORI is straightening up. RICHARD is watching her. She feels his eyes on her.)

LORI: I'm sorry. I don't know what came over me.

RICHARD: You will apologize, won't you?

LORI: The next time he comes in.

RICHARD: I've got his number. Why don't you call him?

LORI: Is that an order?

RICHARD: I'm only making a suggestion. We are talking about our Sam.

LORI: He's not my Sam.

RICHARD: I thought you liked him. The two of you were always laughing.

LORI: I tolerate him. And my laughter drowns out the sound of his voice.

RICHARD: You hurt him. That's not like you.

LORI: That fat queen is as hard as nails.

RICHARD: That's not true.

LORI: He's some pathetic throw-back. Today, I couldn't stand looking at him. I couldn't stand listening to him. And I have to tell you, hated touching him. Why a man would want to act like that...

RICHARD: He's a beautiful queen.

LORI: Where's the beauty?

RICHARD: He's totally reinvented himself.

LORI: That's one useless invention.

RICHARD: Lori, I know you're very angry...

LORI: Don't treat me like a talk show guest.

RICHARD: I can't have you insulting our customers.

LORI: I only told him he should get himself a real life.

RICHARD: He has a real life.

LORI: I shouldn't work here anymore. Stop booking me. I'll finish out the week and that will be it.

RICHARD: Let's talk about this.

LORI: No. I want out of here. I hate it. And I'm beginning to hate you.

RICHARD: Please, don't tell me that.

LORI: Don't give me your martyred "I'm a good person" look. (Furious) Why don't you call me a bitch? Why aren't you yelling at me? Are you frightened of

me? Or are you consumed with so much pity for me
that you can't think? What is it?

RICHARD: You're my friend, and you need help.

LORI: And that stupid, fat queen doesn't?

(They just stare at each other. Then...)

RICHARD: Okay...just finish out the week.

(End of scene)

Scene Ten

(SUSAN's apartment. Later that evening)

*(SUSAN and NICHOLAS are eating their cake quietly.
PAUL looks quite out of it.)*

SUSAN: *(To PAUL)* You haven't touched your cake.

PAUL: I'm not very hungry.

NICHOLAS: Paul, are you all right?

PAUL: I'm fine. It's just that I haven't been sleeping well.
They say that happens when you stop drinking.

NICHOLAS: But it's been a couple of months now.

PAUL: I guess sometimes it takes longer.

NICHOLAS: Paul, you're not sick, are you?

PAUL: No. Why? Do you want me sick?

NICHOLAS: Where the hell did that come from?

PAUL: Sorry. I'm just tired tonight. Forgive me, really.

SUSAN: *(After a moment)* We have news.

PAUL: Yes?

NICHOLAS: We're pregnant.

PAUL: Oh, God...I'm so happy for you guys.

SUSAN: You're going to be Uncle Paul.

NICHOLAS: And we just found out that it's going to be a boy.

PAUL: Then you've been pregnant for some time. Why haven't you told me?

NICHOLAS: *(Indicating SUSAN)* I have no idea.

SUSAN: You've been depressed. I wanted to wait for a happier time.

PAUL: Have you thought of any names?

SUSAN: Not yet. Any suggestions?

PAUL: How about Kevin?

NICHOLAS: I don't want to name him after somebody who's died.

PAUL: You're bound to. At least this would be somebody you knew. And he was your best friend.

SUSAN: Kevin is a lovely name. I hadn't thought of that.

PAUL: Well, consider it.

NICHOLAS: *(To PAUL)* Is this some kind of test?

PAUL: Maybe. Why didn't you tell me about the baby?

NICHOLAS: Here we go. Tonight's going to be about you.

SUSAN: Guys!

NICHOLAS: *(To PAUL)* I'm sorry, it's just...I'm worried about you.

PAUL: Why is that hard for me to believe?

SUSAN: Is this about to turn into a pissing contest?

NICHOLAS: *(Ignoring SUSAN)* Look, I just want to get a little joy back in our lives. Remember it? We're going to have a baby. Aren't you happy about that?

PAUL: Of course. What the hell do you think of me?

NICHOLAS: Well, the truth is...you seem to be getting worse. Maybe you're not getting the right kind of help.

PAUL: *(To* NICHOLAS*)* What do you mean worse?

SUSAN: Hello?!?

NICHOLAS: Never mind. Forget it.

SUSAN: Thank you.

PAUL: No, I want to hear.

SUSAN: Why are you guys doing this?

PAUL: I want to hear what your husband has to say. His opinions are usually so guarded.

NICHOLAS: You've turned into one hell of a self-centered son-of-a-bitch. That wasn't very guarded, was it?

*(*PAUL *applauds.)*

PAUL: How long have you wanted to say that?

NICHOLAS: For a while now.

PAUL: And you can be one hell of a cold bastard.

NICHOLAS: And how long have you wanted to say that?

PAUL: As a matter of fact...years.

NICHOLAS: Really. And I was under the impression that...during those years...we were buddies. Close. Two people who really cared for each other. I guess it was all bullshit.

SUSAN: I want to thank you both for taking this happy day and ruining it for me. You both can share the crown for cold and self-centered bastards. Couldn't you both just have thought of the baby and me tonight?

NICHOLAS: I'm sorry, Susan. I just can't put up with him right now.

PAUL: Him? I'm still in the room.

NICHOLAS: You are getting weirder than bat shit.

PAUL: I better get going. Who wants to be around bat shit.

(PAUL *gets up and heads out the door.*)

(SUSAN *and* NICHOLAS *just stare at each other for a moment.*)

SUSAN: I might never forgive you.

NICHOLAS: Why aren't you running after him?

(*End of scene*)

Scene Eleven

(*The Street. Night*)

(DANIEL *faces the audience.*)

DANIEL: I'm following him all the time now. It's become an addiction. I think in terms of addictions these days. See, I'm going to A A. Well...I've never had a problem with alcohol, but he goes there. So I go there too. Pills are my thing. So much simpler. I sit near him. Never too close. Trying to get to know him. He doesn't look well. It's the dead boy. The dead boy must be haunting him. Crying out for the years he was robbed of. The dead boy is eating his soul. I've thought of going to him and telling him..."I'm the witness. I saw it all. You can talk to me. We're twins in this." I want him so bad...this Paul. He never shares at meetings. He just sits there... tuned out. Nobody pays much attention to me there. They have to be polite. But they erase me. Like people do when they pass me on the street. I want to say to him... "You're walking free because of me. Can I come home with you tonight? Can I kiss you? My kisses will be so deep that I'll suck the dead boy out of you." I could blackmail him. But I won't, because

I'm falling in love. Don't laugh. I am. You know how I
fall asleep? I tell myself this story. One morning I wake
up, and I'm this gym rat. Great body. Big arms. The
big-dicked black man that those white boys dream
about. He sees me. And this time, he follows me. Asks
me to lunch. We eat in a place with tablecloths. We sip
wine...I have to change that part, because he's in A A.
So he sips some foreign bottled water. We tell secrets.
I tell him how my stepfather beat me. Burned me. Tried
to kill the queer in me. How I ran away at twelve. How
I worked the streets. How I was passed around. How
I pray there is no God. Because if He exists, He would
have to be a sick fuck to watch a boy being burned by
his new father. I'd tell him things. I'd tell him about
Mister Jarowski who I thought was kind but... What
a bastard he turned out to be. Lived with him for two
and a half years when I was so young. I was his project.
It started out like a "fairy," fairy tale. A high. He
educated me. And I was a fast learner. I've always
had pretensions. Too fast a learner really. Because...
one morning he realized what he really wanted
was a young thug or just a little black boy... Clichés...
clichés... This country is built on them. Swims in them.
Life can be brutal. But we cope, don't we? *(Pauses)*
I'd tell Paul things ...someone has to know. I follow
him. He's my life now. Maybe some day he'll look back
and see me.

(End of scene)

Scene Twelve

(LORI's kitchen. Evening)

*(FATHER JAMES, wearing just his pants, is at the table
drinking a beer. LORI picks up a cup of coffee from the table.)*

FATHER JAMES: Doesn't that keep you up?

LORI: I have pills now.

FATHER JAMES: So what are you going to do now?

LORI: Maybe I should go on a long trip. See some of this country.

FATHER JAMES: By yourself? Won't that be lonely?

LORI: Then maybe I should go on a cruise. Or move to Florida. Tampa. My sister is there.

FATHER JAMES: That might be a good idea. Start a new life.

LORI: So I'd leave here, and you wouldn't care?

FATHER JAMES: Of course I would. I'd visit. As often as I could.

LORI: You'll find somebody else to "take care of your priestly needs".

FATHER JAMES: (Sarcastically) Yeah. Within five minutes. There's already a waiting list.

LORI: In a way, you're ideal for a middle-aged woman who is used to being alone. You're dependable. You stick to a schedule. And you're never around long enough to mess up an apartment.

FATHER JAMES: Maybe you should write my ad for the church bulletin.

LORI: Richard says I need help. I hurt this faggot's feelings. But what I really wanted to do was scald his head with the dye.

FATHER JAMES: That's not like you.

LORI: I'm enjoying the hatred. It's giving me something else to feel.

FATHER JAMES: Please, see somebody.

LORI: He's a platinum blonde this season. Useless and ugly in this frightening world.

FATHER JAMES: You don't know that.

LORI: And he'll probably live to be a hundred. Nothing bad will ever happen to him. Except for the little soap operas he'll create for himself.

FATHER JAMES: Lori...

LORI: In Florida, do you think, finally, you could spend the night?

FATHER JAMES: Most definitely.

LORI: *(After a moment)* Maybe I should see somebody. I am getting paranoid. I keep thinking that I'm being followed.

(DANIEL appears on the stage near them. He is on the street. He faces the audience.)

DANIEL: He's following her. Not all the time. Like I follow him. I bet she'll catch him following her before he catches me following him. You see, I'm invisible to the world.

(End of scene)

Scene Thirteen

(A bar)

(RICHARD is trying to look cheerful, as if he is enjoying himself. PAUL walks over to him. PAUL is drinking bottled water.)

PAUL: Hi there.

RICHARD: Hello.

PAUL: It's kind of empty tonight, isn't it?

RICHARD: I wouldn't know.

PAUL: Well, look around.

RICHARD: What I meant was I don't usually come here. So I wouldn't know if it were more crowded than usual or less. I'm not really a bar person.

PAUL: Everybody says that.

RICHARD: Well, I mean it.

PAUL: Is my bar banter blowing it?

RICHARD: Blowing what?

PAUL: I wanted to make a good impression on you.

RICHARD: Why was that?

PAUL: So maybe you'd come home with me.

RICHARD: No, thank you.

PAUL: Can we start again? I'm really out of practice. I haven't been in a bar for a while. Rusty.

RICHARD: Rusty, I won't be coming home with you.

PAUL: It's Paul. What I meant was I was rusty at this kind of thing. You're Richard, right?

RICHARD: How did you know?

PAUL: I'm clairvoyant. I know people's names, ages... that's a real curse...and their favorite *I Love Lucy* episode. No, really...I've been to your salon. As a matter of fact, I was meaning to drop by to ask you about that woman who used to work there. I loved the way she cut my hair.

RICHARD: What woman?

PAUL: I forgot her name.

RICHARD: That's a handicap for someone who's clairvoyant.

PAUL: Right. I believe she was the mother of that boy who was killed.

RICHARD: Lori.

PAUL: Right.

RICHARD: She quit.

PAUL: That's too bad. How's she doing?

RICHARD: Not too well.

PAUL: I guess that's to be expected. What is she like? Does she have other children? Was she close to her son?

RICHARD: I don't want to talk about her.

PAUL: Sorry. I was kind of fascinated by her. You know...once upon a time people thought I was charming.

RICHARD: Once upon a time we all were. Another time. Another universe.

PAUL: Boy, it is empty in here tonight. The internet has killed the weekday bar trade. The boys can get exactly what they want online. The internet is one big take-out menu. You're very attractive. *(Jokingly)* For an older guy.

RICHARD: Thanks.

PAUL: You look married. I bet you've got a boyfriend.

RICHARD: I had one. He died.

PAUL: Oh, those dead boyfriends. They're all over the place. I've got one of them too.

RICHARD: Sorry.

PAUL: Me too.

RICHARD: Let's not swap war stories.

PAUL: Definitely not. I'm not used to this.

RICHARD: Being aggressive or talking?

PAUL: Being in a bar without drinking. I shouldn't be here.

RICHARD: I see. How's it feel?

PAUL: Like I don't know myself. I've got to get out of here.

RICHARD: You're not really bothering me. In fact...

PAUL: Sorry. But suddenly all I'm really wanting is a beer. Craving it. I didn't think this would happen to me. Look how I'm sweating. But let me give you my number?

RICHARD: I doubt I'd be calling.

(PAUL writes out his number on a piece of paper.)

PAUL: You never know. Some night you might be interested in war stories. Or maybe...some night... you'll have an erotic dream about me...

RICHARD: I don't have erotic dreams anymore.

PAUL: Like I said, you never know. Please...take it. I can't believe how I'm shaking.

(PAUL, who is trying to hold it together, hands RICHARD his number. RICHARD takes it.)

PAUL: Thanks. You never know.

(End of scene)

Scene Fourteen

(A street. Day)

(DANIEL is facing the audience.)

DANIEL: He goes to New Jersey a lot these days. I don't like going there. It's hard getting change in Jersey. So I wait by the PATH train until he gets back. While I wait, I chat with friends. It's our latest hang-out. Then I follow him home. Maybe he's not the sad sack I think he is. Maybe he's not just following that woman. Maybe

he's got a Jersey boy on the side. You know the type.
Can't dress. Closeted. Bad hair. And hotter than we
ever want to admit. He doesn't go to our A A meeting
anymore. So I don't get to sit near him. I feel like one of
those women on Doctor Phil. You know, those gals that
fall in love with convicted killers. I mean, what's that
about? But here I am stalking my little murderer. My
little sweetheart. My little "I'm an alcoholic" Paul.

(End of scene)

Scene Fifteen

(A park bench. Day)

*(LORI is looking at a newspaper. PAUL, who has been
watching her, approaches. He tries to mask his nerves.)*

PAUL: *(Tentatively)* Well, hello.

LORI: *(Suspiciously)* Do I know you?

PAUL: Lori, right? You used to cut my hair.
In the Village.

LORI: Sorry, I don't remember you.

PAUL: Paul.

LORI: Sorry.

PAUL: You're not there anymore, are you?

LORI: No.

PAUL: Are you at some other shop now?

LORI: A beauty parlor around here. It's just women.

PAUL: Is it easier?

LORI: What do you mean?

PAUL: Are they easier than gay guys?

LORI: They're about the same.

PAUL: Fussy, right?

LORI: That's one way of putting it.

PAUL: I live in the Village. But I go to mass at Saint Anthony's.

LORI: You come all the way over here to go to mass?

PAUL: I like that church. It's low-key and private.
(He joins her on the bench.)

LORI: It was my parish. Now, I'm ambivalent about the whole thing. I don't remember you. And I usually remember my clients.

PAUL: Maybe I wasn't that fussy.

LORI: Then I'd really remember you.

PAUL: It's nice to see you again. Are you going to mass tonight?

LORI: No.

PAUL: I am. It seems I'm needing the church more and more.

LORI: Why?

PAUL: I lost my lover over a year ago.

LORI: So you're looking for a reason?

PAUL: Maybe.

LORI: Or you're hoping you'll see him again?

PAUL: Oh, I don't know about that. That seems too fairy tale-ish to me.

LORI: Yes, that is, isn't it? Then don't you wonder...what's the sense of believing in any of it?

PAUL: It gives you the possibility.

LORI: The possibility? I kind of like that.

PAUL: Are you okay?

LORI: *(Suddenly angry)* You know about my son, don't you?

PAUL: Yes.

LORI: Damn you! Are you from some activist group?

PAUL: No. Really, no!

LORI: Don't you people understand? I don't want to have anything to do with you.

PAUL: I'm not part of any group. I'm not.

LORI: They send me letters...call me...I don't want anything to do with them.

PAUL: That's understandable. They should leave you alone.

LORI: Sure. Like you're doing.

PAUL: *(Getting more nervous)* Sorry. What I was about to say was we can only cut away at our grief in our own way. Chip at it, slowly.

LORI: And how's your "chipping" going?

PAUL: Won't be over. Not in this lifetime. *(He starts crying.)*

LORI: *(After a moment)* You're crying.

PAUL: No big deal. I do it all the time.

LORI: I hate to see boys cry.

PAUL: But we do.

LORI: What I meant was tears frighten me. I worry they'll never stop.

PAUL: I was just...hoping...maybe...I could do something. Help you in some way.

LORI: Why? What are you? Some grief therapist?

PAUL: Hardly. Just another walking train wreck.

LORI: Don't call yourself that.

PAUL: It's almost time for mass. You wouldn't want to come with me? Would you?

LORI: Why would I want to do that?

PAUL: Because there's only reruns on television. And the news is too bleak.

LORI: Times certainly have changed. A few years ago you would have asked me to go for a drink.

PAUL: Can't really do that. I'm not drinking these days.

LORI: So now it's church. Can't handle the excitement.

PAUL: If you get out of hand, I'll restrain you. I'm just looking for company.

LORI: I used to feel comfortable in church. But not anymore. *(Pause)* When you go there, where do you like to sit?

PAUL: In the back.

LORI: Me too.

PAUL: The front for movies.

LORI: Absolutely.

PAUL: The back for church.

LORI: But no church for me right now.

PAUL: Why not?

LORI: Ever since my son was killed, I've become paranoid. Afraid.

PAUL: Of what?

LORI: God.

PAUL: But He's love.

LORI: Is He?

(End of scene)

Scene Sixteen

(The street. Night)

(DANIEL faces the audience.)

DANIEL: He got back late tonight. I almost gave up waiting. Maybe I'm not that loyal a lover. But I ran into Celia. Well, it's really Carl. But when he wears that awful green dress of his...he's Celia. She wanted me to do a job with her. I'm not partial to those kinds of jobs. But it was a quick buck. And she had some nice pills on her. This job was a real easy one. All we had to do is get in a car with this white dude and call him all sorts of names while he took care of himself. Didn't even have to touch him or get touched. We were out of that car in eight minutes with thirty bucks each. I was feeling good when I was following Paul home. Because I knew I was going to get myself a burger with the works. That was until Paul began to shake. Then he vomited. Maybe he's sick. Real sick.

(End of scene)

Scene Seventeen

(PAUL's apartment. Night)

(A candle burns. A few props indicate that the place is a mess. Paper, open food cartons, dirty laundry. PAUL just sits there. A radio plays in the background. A strong knock is heard.)

SUSAN: *(Off-stage)* Paul, I know you're in there. Open up! I'm feeling like a grade-B movie actress. Now, open the fucking door.

(PAUL *slowly gets up and heads for the door.*)

SUSAN: *(Off-stage)* I'll call the police. I swear.

(PAUL *opens the door.*)

SUSAN: You're going for some help whether you want to or not. *(She enters the apartment.)* This place is beginning to smell.

PAUL: Well, hello to you too.

SUSAN: And you're losing weight.

PAUL: I've become a vegetarian.

SUSAN: Since when?

PAUL: A while now.

SUSAN: So you don't eat pig anymore. You've just become one.

PAUL: It's a way to curb violence, isn't it? Not ingesting any more fear and rage.

SUSAN: What are you talking about?

PAUL: I'm trying to be good. I'm trying to live in peace. Do you know how they kill the chickens we eat?

SUSAN: You can't keep living like this.

PAUL: They scream. They cry. They want to live as much as we do.

SUSAN: Shut up!

PAUL: *(After a moment)* I want to be good. We should try to be good. *(Pause)* You're getting big.

SUSAN: Well, I'm due next month. Now, who are we going to call to get you help?

PAUL: I don't want any help!

SUSAN: I know we said we'd never talk about what happened again. But it's not working. Not working at all. I can't get that boy and you out of my head.

PAUL: I don't know what you're talking about!

SUSAN: And look what it's doing to you.

PAUL: I don't know what you're talking about!

SUSAN: *(Pause)* How are you doing for money?

PAUL: I've got some.

SUSAN: You really should go back to work. Don't you miss the library?

PAUL: I quit.

SUSAN: You loved that job.

PAUL: Time for a change.

SUSAN: Oh, for Chrissakes. You're really frightening me. What the hell are you doing with your days?

PAUL: Thinking. Going to church.

SUSAN: But you're an atheist.

PAUL: Don't remind me. I'm trying. I'm trying to believe. I so want to believe. I keep thinking... keep praying. Keep praying. And maybe...maybe a miracle will occur. And suddenly I'll believe in a God. A God whose arms are open to everyone. A God who's embracing all our dead. Now...please...get back to your life and leave your older brother alone.

SUSAN: To do what?

PAUL: To continue his fix-up life.

SUSAN: There has to be something or somebody that can help you.

PAUL: If I could...bring back that boy in the alley and make him love me. Make him love all of us. Good-bye, my little Susie. May your child...

SUSAN: It's a boy.

PAUL: I remember. May his smile be sunshine. May he have your eyes, your kindness... There are many ways to live. I'm in transition. Check with me in a month... a year...two years... *(He walks over to the door and opens it.)* Now, I said good-bye. Go home. You have a chance for happiness.

SUSAN: You can't do this. You can't send me out of your life. It's not going to work. I'm not leaving.

PAUL: I love you more than anything. But you can be one stubborn bitch. *(After a moment)* Well, whatever.

(PAUL walks through the door, leaving a stunned SUSAN.)

(End of scene)

Scene Eighteen

(A church confessional. Late afternoon)

(FATHER JAMES is seated. LORI slowly kneels close to him.)

(Only when the lights widen is it revealed that LORI is in a confessional.)

LORI: *(Making the sign of the cross)* Bless me, Father, for I have sinned.

FATHER JAMES: Lori...

LORI: My last confession was...

FATHER JAMES: We've talked about this. I shouldn't be hearing your confession.

LORI: There's no one else here today.

FATHER JAMES: You shouldn't confess at this church anyway.

LORI: What's with you? You lecture me when I don't come to church. Now that I'm here...

FATHER JAMES: You've waited a long time. Wait another day. Go to Saint Mary Mount Carmel.

LORI: I don't want to. It's you that has to hear it.

FATHER JAMES: This is not a good idea.

LORI: Why? Are you afraid that this will be more intimate than our fucking?

FATHER JAMES: Lori, please...not here.

LORI: I'm sorry, I'm sorry. Don't deny me my confession.

FATHER JAMES: *(After a moment)* If you have to.

LORI: Bless me, Father, for I have sinned. My last confession was six, seven...I don't know...it was years and years ago. I don't know really where to begin.

FATHER JAMES: Why do you feel such a strong need to confess at this moment?

LORI: I feel our Lord has singled me out to suffer.

FATHER JAMES: I know it feels that way. But it's not true.

LORI: I was convinced that God did not exist. That he was a fabrication of our needs. I was comfortable with that idea. Almost happy. But then...I met this stranger and suddenly...there it was. God...exists...and He sent this stranger to me as a punishment. And now, I'm frightened of Him. And frightened of my hate for Him.

FATHER JAMES: Of this stranger?

LORI: Of God!

FATHER JAMES: Lori, now is the time you should be taking refuge in His love.

LORI: Help me. Help me find that love. Look around. What do you see? Beauty? Love?

FATHER JAMES: Yes.

LORI: All I see is His vengeance. Everywhere I look. His punishment. His punishment for all our sins, my sins.

FATHER JAMES: You are not a great sinner. You're good. You were a wonderful mother. Our Lord loves you.

LORI: You are arrogant. They should rip that collar from your neck.

FATHER JAMES: I want you to see a therapist. I want you to call one today.

LORI: I don't need a therapist. I want this idea...this idea of Christ to forgive me. I want to bathe in His light. That light I'm always hearing about, but never seeing. I want you to ask for His forgiveness too.

FATHER JAMES: I love you.

LORI: That's your dick talking.

FATHER JAMES: It's not.

LORI: Don't you believe in God?

FATHER JAMES: Our love did not kill your son.

LORI: What are you doing in the church?

FATHER JAMES: Trying to do some of Christ's work.

LORI: I believe in God, and I'm frightened of Him. My stranger...he's gay. He tells me he believes it all. And that he truly believes that God is love.

FATHER JAMES: If He exists, He is.

LORI: This stranger likes me. He wants me to go to church with him. He thinks he's bringing me comfort.

The night my son was killed...earlier that evening...
how my boy and I laughed. I was making fun of
Richard and the fussy little cookies he brought into the
shop. I minced around the room. We roared. Richard
doesn't mince. A few hours later my son gets murdered
by somebody who hates gay people. What an enormous
sense of humor our Creator has. How He must be
laughing at me. He sent me this stranger...Mister Good
Deeds. Mister Gay Angel. His presence, his spirituality
are razor blades slicing my fucking heart.

FATHER JAMES: Let me take you home. I'll pray with
you. Hold you. Whatever you want.

LORI: Why am I talking to you? You can't help me.
You can't deliver this God...this Lord to me. Mary,
she's a mother. She'll help me.

(LORI *pulls out a rosary and starts rocking back and forth.*
FATHER JAMES *runs out of the confessional to help* LORI.)

LORI: "Hail Mary, full of grace, the Lord is with thee..."

FATHER JAMES: Please, stop this!

LORI: (*Vehemently*) You must never touch me again!
Never! "...blessed art thou among women..."

FATHER JAMES: Did I do this to you?

LORI: (*Getting more and more hysterical*) You...me...
we're only His instruments. He did it. He did it.
"...and blessed is the fruit of thy womb...Jesus...
Holy Mary, mother of God, pray for us sinners now
and at the hour of our death. Amen."

END OF ACT ONE

ACT TWO

Scene Nineteen

(PAUL's *apartment. Night*)

(RICHARD *is quite nervous.* PAUL *seems relaxed.*)

RICHARD: I just took a chance calling you tonight.
I'm surprised you remembered me after all this time.

PAUL: I'm glad I answered the phone.

RICHARD: I don't usually do things like this.

PAUL: Like what?

RICHARD: Call someone I hardly know up and...
you know. You look so pensive.

PAUL: I'm wondering what you look like without
your clothes.

RICHARD: You move fast.

PAUL: I don't think you came here to discuss Proust.

RICHARD: Not Proust. But the use of irony in Jackie
Collins.

PAUL: Touché. My people skills deteriorate with each
day.

RICHARD: I haven't had sex in a long time.

PAUL: Neither have I...really.

RICHARD: That's hard to believe.

PAUL: Why?

RICHARD: You come on like Attila.

PAUL: *(Laughing)* Kevin would have roared if he'd heard you say that. He thought of me as a bit uptight and shy.

RICHARD: Was he your lover?

PAUL: Yes. My dead lover.

RICHARD: Mine was John.

PAUL: Gay boys have so much in common. Our love for divas and dead boyfriends.

RICHARD: Did I mention I was negative?

PAUL: Ditto.

RICHARD: Strange, isn't it? I don't know if this is going to work. I'm just too nervous.

PAUL: Well, let's find out if it's like riding a bicycle.

RICHARD: I just can't jump into it.

PAUL: Don't you like sex?

RICHARD: I'm obsessed with it. Masturbate way too much for somebody my age. I'm one hell of a weird gay guy. It's been five years since John's death. And in all that time, I've only had sex twice. Both were pathetic disasters. But my fantasies have gotten more and more bizarre. I mean, I used to be very vanilla.

PAUL: Don't know what I am anymore. Why don't you tell me one of those bizarre fantasies? Why don't we go there tonight?

RICHARD: We're all damaged goods.

PAUL: True, but let's not think about that. Let's try to forget about everything for the next hour or two.

RICHARD: Two? That's optimistic.

PAUL: I'm trying. Whisper one of your fantasies to me. I'll create it for you. Weave it. I'll enter your mind and take it over. Tell you what to think. That way I can stop thinking too. Whisper one to me. The darker, the better. Go there. Let's go there together.

RICHARD: What a relief...to forget...just for a little while.

PAUL: Talk to me.

(RICHARD *moves close to* PAUL *and starts whispering.*)

(*End of scene*)

Scene Twenty

(SUSAN's *apartment. Night*)

(SUSAN *is sitting in her robe. She is no longer pregnant.* NICHOLAS *comes into the room.*)

NICHOLAS: You should get some sleep.

SUSAN: He doesn't have an answering machine anymore.

NICHOLAS: You know, the baby's going to be up in a couple of hours.

SUSAN: I need to grow up. I'm a mother now. I have a son to take care of.

NICHOLAS: You're a wonderful mother.

SUSAN: But not a very good wife.

NICHOLAS: I didn't say that.

SUSAN: Without Paul, I feel like I just lost my mother and father again.

NICHOLAS: You look tired. Please come to bed.

SUSAN: Would you hold me until I fall asleep?

NICHOLAS: Of course.

SUSAN: Ethan's a happy baby, isn't he?

NICHOLAS: He does love to smile.

SUSAN: I want him to be happy as long as he can.

NICHOLAS: That's our job.

SUSAN: And what a wonderful one that is. *(She picks up the phone and starts dialing.)* Let me try one more time.

NICHOLAS: Susan, no.

SUSAN: Just one more time.

(On the other side of the stage, PAUL sits by the ringing phone in his apartment.)

SUSAN: Paul, pick up the phone. Come on.

(PAUL does not pick up the phone.)

PAUL: Oh, little Susie. You've got to give me up.

(PAUL just sits. When the phone stops ringing, RICHARD knocks on the door.)

RICHARD: *(Off-stage)* Paul, it's Richard.

(PAUL waits a second before he decides to go over to the door and open it. RICHARD enters with a bouquet of flowers. He hands the flowers to PAUL.)

RICHARD: Hi.

PAUL: Thank you.

RICHARD: I've called, but you're never home. And you don't have a machine.

PAUL: Which seems to be a felony in this city.

RICHARD: Didn't mean it as a criticism. Am I interrupting anything?

PAUL: No.

RICHARD: I just want to tell you I really enjoyed the other night.

PAUL: The sex was incredible.

RICHARD: It certainly was. But it was more than that.

PAUL: Don't spoil it. Please, don't.

RICHARD: How?

PAUL: By telling me you felt a connection. That you felt
something other than sex.

RICHARD: I wasn't about to book the church. But I did
feel something. Thought you did too. My gaydar must
be burnt out. Boy, do I feel foolish.

PAUL: No need to. I'm glad you're here. I'd like to hear
another of your fantasies. I'd like to act it out with you.
I need to forget again. Like we did the other night.
A drug. That's what our sex was like. A drug...I didn't
even know I was craving. But there is nothing else I can
ever have.

RICHARD: Why not?

PAUL: My dead. They've robbed me of all my love.

RICHARD: Your lover?

PAUL: And others.

RICHARD: You're just afraid.

PAUL: No psychobabble. Tell me a wilder fantasy than
the one we did the other night. Tell me what it is you
want done to you, and I'll do it. I'll do almost anything.

RICHARD: I'm sorry, but no.

PAUL: Please! I really need to forget tonight. Go really
dark.

RICHARD: I can't.

PAUL: You want to. I can tell. You're getting that
"shy, bad boy, should I do it, should I not" look. We

can forget again for a few hours. Wouldn't that be wonderful? Come on, tell me.

RICHARD: No.

PAUL: Why not?

RICHARD: My heart's not dead yet.

PAUL: Lucky, lucky you. But some night. Some horny, lonely night. And that night will come. When there is no thought of connections. No thought of love. When you are drowning in your fantasies. When you're consumed with them. Please, don't be embarrassed. Just give me a call. I'll be here. Waiting.

RICHARD: No. I'm so sorry.

(RICHARD *kisses* PAUL *on the forehead.* PAUL *pushes him away.* RICHARD *leaves, and* PAUL *crumbles.*)

(End of scene)

Scene Twenty-one

(The street. Night)

*(*DANIEL *faces the audience.)*

DANIEL: Oooh, I am feeling evil today. One pissed-off queen. I go to my meeting. And he's not there again. What's that about? I know...I shouldn't feel stood up by somebody who doesn't know I'm waiting. But I do. You know, we're supposed to be a nicer city after September eleventh. And we were. For a while. But today, this lady and her baby... There are so many babies around lately. Everybody is getting them. Middle-aged people, old people even, young people, gay people, lesbian people... Everybody wants a baby these days. It used to be a home entertainment center. Then a computer. Now, it's babies. Anyway, this lady...an older type...and her baby were almost killed.

A car turned a corner way too fast. The carriage flew out of the lady's hand. She fell. The carriage toppled over. The baby hit the concrete. Was screaming. I ran so fast to pick up the baby so a car wouldn't smash him. She yelled, *(Screaming)* "Stay away from him!" *(After a moment)* She didn't want me to touch him. Luckily, someone else scooped up the baby. I wanted to spit on her. But I just walked away. With a little bit of attitude. Well, with high attitude. *(Screaming)* "Stay away from him!"

(End of scene)

Scene Twenty-two

(The street. Day)

(LORI suddenly turns and faces PAUL. DANIEL stands apart from them.)

LORI: It is you. What are you doing?

PAUL: *(Acting surprised)* Why, hello.

LORI: Have you been following me?

DANIEL: *(To the audience)* He's caught. But no one is noticing me. Invisible.

PAUL: No. I didn't realize it was you.

LORI: I thought I saw you yesterday.

PAUL: You couldn't have. I was in Manhattan all day.

DANIEL: He's lying. I followed him to Jersey.

LORI: I thought I was being paranoid. But somebody's been following me. And it's been you. Why?

PAUL: You're being silly. Let's go get some coffee.

LORI: Do you know something about my son? I sensed that from the first day I met you. You were never a client of mine. Tell me what you know!

PAUL: I know nothing. Really.

DANIEL: Except you saw him take his final breath. And you matched his hate. Maybe even exceeded it.

LORI: I want to know now.

PAUL: Know what?

LORI: Oh my God...do you know who killed him?

PAUL: No!

LORI: Were you a friend of his?

PAUL: I never met him.

LORI: That's not true. I know that's not true.

PAUL: I better go.

LORI: You move one step away from me, and I'll start screaming. How did you know my son?

PAUL: I didn't know him.

LORI: Did you meet him in that bar? Had he been there before?

PAUL: No!

LORI: Oh...it can't be that.... You didn't?... Did you... did you love him?

PAUL: What?

LORI: You did. You loved him.

PAUL: You don't know what you're talking about.

LORI: Was he...? My son...was he gay?

PAUL: You told me he wasn't.

LORI: But he was, wasn't he? How stupid, how blind. I swear I didn't know.

PAUL: You know he wasn't.

LORI: You're lying. I can see it in your eyes. Look at you. Wanting to be close to me. You loved my son. I can feel it. Were you both in love? Was he in love too?

DANIEL: The dead boy's here. He'll take his revenge.

LORI: Did he ever talk about me? What did he say? Come with me. Tell me about my son.

PAUL: I can't. This is wrong.

LORI: I'll beg. I'll get down on my knees. Right here on the street.

PAUL: I'll never bother you again. I swear it.

(LORI *gets down on her knees.*)

LORI: Please...

PAUL: Don't do this!

LORI: Come home with me. You're as sad as I am. You ache for him too, don't you?

PAUL: Please...get up!

LORI: We can talk. We can even cry together. Tell me about him. I want to know.

PAUL: *(Shaking)* What have I done?!?

LORI: Come with me.

PAUL: All right, all right. If that's what you want.

LORI: Oh, yes. There's so much you have to tell me.

(PAUL *helps* LORI *up.* DANIEL *watches them.*)

DANIEL: The dead boy.

(DANIEL *walks away.* LORI *and* PAUL *take a few steps and sit in two chairs facing each other.*)

(The scene melts into LORI's *kitchen.* LORI *hands* PAUL *a photograph.)*

LORI: You can have this picture of him.

PAUL: I couldn't.

LORI: No, really. I want you to have it. Will would have wanted me to give it to you. You sure I can't get you anything? A little something to drink. A cup of coffee? A soda?

PAUL: No...no, thank you.

LORI: Did he have lots of gay friends?

PAUL: I don't think so.

LORI: He was new to it all, wasn't he?

PAUL: I believe so.

LORI: Must have been. I had no inkling. Not the slightest.

PAUL: It's hard for young sons to tell their mothers.

LORI: And I made it harder.

PAUL: Probably not.

LORI: Oh, yes. Where did you meet? Was it in that bar?

PAUL: No, in a coffee shop.

LORI: How long ago?

PAUL: Just a few months before...

LORI: But you loved him?

(There is an awkward silence.)

LORI: Please...tell me. Yes?

PAUL: Yes.

LORI: His smile. It was wonderful, wasn't it? That picture captures it. Don't you think so?

PAUL: Yes. He was handsome.

LORI: He was, wasn't he? I took the picture. About a
month before... We were in Atlantic City. Did a little
gambling. I'm sure he told you. Please, don't be shy.
Talk to me about him. You don't know what it means to
me. When I buried him, how I wished there were more
people there who loved him. It's probably my fault. I'm
not too social. Too guarded. I have a small family...just
a few friends. He seemed popular at school though. At
least, that's what I thought. But only a few of his friends
came to the church. Young people...they avoid funerals,
don't they? Were the two of you serious about each
other? Were you making plans for the future?

PAUL: I don't know how serious he was. There was an
age difference. You're not upset to find out he was gay?

LORI: I don't know. I'm just happy to talk to someone
else who loved him.

PAUL: I see.

LORI: Mothers love talking about their sons. All
mothers think their sons are geniuses. It's ridiculous.
But we do. When you guys are little and helpless,
we have such fantasies about your futures. What were
your mother's dreams for you?

PAUL: I wouldn't know. She died when I was young.

LORI: How sad.

PAUL: Yes, it was. Very, very sad.

LORI: What was she like? Do you remember?

PAUL: Vaguely. Every once in a while, on those "can't-
sleep nights," I wonder what my life would have been
like if my mother lived. I wonder who I would have
been. How differently I would have handled things.

LORI: When Will was a baby, I was convinced that
when he grew up he would discover the cure for

cancer. Or be a senator. Or maybe invent something
that would make him hideously rich. But he turned
out to be just a regular guy. But regular in so many
wonderful ways. *(Pause)* How I wish he would have
been comfortable enough to tell me he was gay.
I would have gotten used to it. I'm just glad he was
loved. Now, you don't have to follow me anymore.
We can be friends. Good friends. Because now I know.

PAUL: *(From his soul)* I am sorry.

LORI: Your mother would have been proud of you.
Because you're kind.

PAUL: *(Crying)* Forgive me. Please...forgive me.

(LORI takes PAUL in her arms.)

LORI: You have a long life ahead of you. You'll fall in
love again.

PAUL: No.

LORI: You will. But I want you to promise me
something. That you won't forget him.

PAUL: I won't. Ever.

LORI: That picture. It does capture him, doesn't it?

(End of scene)

Scene Twenty-three

(The street. Night)

*(DANIEL faces the audience. However, in a dim light
LORI can be seen still holding PAUL.)*

DANIEL: It's the dead boy. He's doing this to us.
We are all waiting. Waiting for something that
will never happen. My Paul waits for the mother's
forgiveness. I know the lie he tells himself. One I'm

very familiar with. That if he's near her that possibility
exists. I wait for my Paul's tongue to slip into my
mouth, but only after he tells me he loves me. Yes,
I want him to love me. And the dead boy...he waits
for his life to come back. So we all wait. For something
we know will never happen.

(End of scene)

Scene Twenty-four

(PAUL's *apartment and* LORI's *apartment. Day)*

(On one side of the stage is PAUL's *apartment. On the other
side is* LORI's. *The scene shifts abruptly from one apartment
to the other.)*

(SUSAN *is with an agitated* PAUL.)

(FATHER JAMES *is with an agitated* LORI.)

SUSAN: *(To* PAUL*)* You called. I'm so happy. Do you
have any idea how much I've missed you?

FATHER JAMES: *(to* LORI*)* You have no idea how I've
missed you.

LORI: My son was gay.

FATHER JAMES: What are you talking about?

PAUL: His mother. I've been following her. I want to
take care of her, comfort her. I want her to love me.
Then maybe I can sleep at night. That's why I told her.

SUSAN: You confessed?

FATHER JAMES: I don't believe it.

LORI: I've met his lover. He sat right here with me.

FATHER JAMES: It's not true.

PAUL: No, I didn't confess. And it wasn't because I was
protecting myself. It would have brought no comfort to

her. That's what I have to do now. Bring her comfort.
That's got to be my purpose in life. A confession
would have caused her more pain. I believe that. Really.
And her feelings...they must come first. No...she thinks
I was her son's lover. I just went along with it.

SUSAN: That is cruel and insane!

PAUL: Insane...yes. But not cruel! No, not cruel. She was
happy someone loved her son.

SUSAN: How could you do that?

LORI: My poor boy...he was wonderful at pretending,
wasn't he? And I know why he had to do it.

PAUL: She is so alone. She needs somebody. She needs
somebody to take care of her. To talk to her about her
son.

SUSAN: Not you!

PAUL: I have to give her something. Something back.

SUSAN: That is impossible.

PAUL: I've got to try.

LORI: All my little fag jokes about Richard. I didn't
really mean them. You know that. But what did they
sound like to my son?

FATHER JAMES: You've been looking for a way to blame
yourself for his death. Now, stop it!

PAUL: Being near her is my punishment. It's my karma.
We know I have to be punished. You can't get away
with what I did.

SUSAN: Paul, leave town. Start a new life.

FATHER JAMES: (Emphatically) You can't see this man
anymore.

LORI: I have to see him. It's my punishment. He's my
penance.

FATHER JAMES: Move to Florida. Be with your sister.

LORI: No. God has other plans for me.

FATHER JAMES: God has nothing to do with this. You are about to create your own hell.

LORI: I'm going to try to love that man.

FATHER JAMES: You know nothing about him.

LORI: I'll learn.

PAUL: I'll do all he would have done for her.

SUSAN: You're not her son. Go away. Someplace peaceful and beautiful. Rest. You need rest. I'll help you.

PAUL: No. I have things to do here. I have a purpose now.

SUSAN: Paul, please, come here.

FATHER JAMES: Lori, let me hold you. Just hold you.

LORI: We shouldn't.

FATHER JAMES: We should. Oh yes, we should.

(SUSAN *is seated.* PAUL *goes over to her, kneels down, and places his head on her lap.*)

(LORI *goes over to* FATHER JAMES. *He embraces her.*)

SUSAN: *(Stroking his hair)* One of the reasons you wouldn't go to the police was Kevin, wasn't it?

PAUL: The answer is "no" to what you've always wanted to ask. No, I did not help him die. I know Nicholas believes I did. I was supposed to. He wanted me to. "When it's the right time, you'll help me, won't you, Paul?" But I didn't. I was too much of a coward. His blue eyes glared at me with such hate. I watched him. I watched him suffer. And I did nothing. I wish I had helped him, my Kevin. Then maybe he would have died looking at me with love.

SUSAN: He loved you.

PAUL: Not those last five days.

FATHER JAMES: Your son loved you. He did. Take that memory with you and start a new life. One that has possibilities for a future.

LORI: Are you saying good-bye to me?

FATHER JAMES: With me...all your life promises is more loneliness.

LORI: And without you?

SUSAN: Why did you go to that alley?

PAUL: I had to. I would find myself there before spending an evening with you guys. Or after. It was my antidote to your happiness. It was my way not to hate you. I would have something. In the alley I would get close to men. The only way I could. Some nights, it would be beyond boring. But other nights, the alley would be filled with hope and youth and sweat. Even the old war horses on such a night would radiate youth. On such a night...in the alley...you could forget everything but the hunt. In the alley...you have no history. You're only a pair of eyes...a cute face... a beautiful dick...an inviting mouth...perfect lips. On the night I met the dead boy...the alley was all too real...pathetic. It was chilly. And it was just us there. I felt old and sad. I should have left. But I didn't. He looked over. A smile. He whipped his dick out, stroked it a bit, and then began the talk. "Do you like this, fag?" I was so disappointed. S/M talk in the alley? Get real, kid. But he meant it. He spit hate. It was no game. Then he walked over and shoved me. I slapped him. He called me a little girl. Making fun of my slap. And then the blows came. And limp wrist little Paulie flew into a rage. I wouldn't stop. He became everyone who ever demeaned me...us...my dead brothers. I didn't stop

until he joined them. Until he joined my dead. And I
added more violence to this world. Who am I, Susan?

LORI: Why don't you take off that collar and come with
me?

FATHER JAMES: You have no idea how much I love you.

LORI: But you love the idea of God more.

FATHER JAMES: Yes.

PAUL: Who am I?

(End of scene)

Scene Twenty-five

(A street. Day)

(DANIEL faces the audience.)

DANIEL: *(To the audience)* If I don't seem so bubbly
today, it's because I'm kind of sad. You know that
Sunday night sad. That back to school tomorrow sad.
That end of summer sad. I'm having one of those days
of missing people who ain't here no more. I miss my
mama. I miss her real bad today. She used to sing,
my mama. Had a real pretty voice. Well, she used to
sing until she married him. That bastard. She met her
grave way too early, my mama did. Leaving me with
him. Yeah...I miss her. A whole lot. I don't sing. I don't
like listening to other people sing. It makes me lonely.
It fills me with missing. I miss my brother, Larry. He
loved me. Didn't care that I was queer. But he loved his
"happy times" more. Those "happy times" the needle
gave him. Sometimes I talk to him at night. Tell him
about my day. Tell him about Paul. I miss Paul too.
I don't see him so much anymore. How I love him.
I shouldn't have started following him. Gave me
something to do though. But pretending to be in love

and then talking myself into it... I didn't need more missing. But we all need somebody to love, don't we? And we need to be loved. That's much rarer these days. I miss those people who used to love me. I'd like to be held tonight. Do you have any idea how long it's been since I've been held? *(Pause)* In the meantime...pills. I'm gonna get me some nice pills tonight.

(End of scene)

Scene Twenty-six

(PAUL's *apartment. Evening)*

(SUSAN *is with* PAUL.)

PAUL: You told him.

SUSAN: I had to.

PAUL: How I wish you hadn't. On top of everything else...now, he'll be afraid of me.

SUSAN: He thinks I love you more than I love him.

PAUL: I'm sorry. He probably wishes I had died instead of Kevin.

SUSAN: That's not true. Kevin's death scared him. It was the first person he ever lost. I shouldn't have left the apartment tonight. I do think I love him though.

PAUL: You do.

SUSAN: You say that because you want me to. But I wanted to be with you. I'm like one of those women you hear about who get married, but will always put Mommy and Daddy first. Who never really leave home. *(To* PAUL*)* Hi, Mommy... Hi, Daddy.

PAUL: Little Susie, it's time you left home. Go to him. Be happy.

SUSAN: *(Dramatically)* "Who's happy?"

PAUL: What?

SUSAN: Oskar Werner, "Ship of Fools." We once watched that movie with Daddy on television. For days afterwards, we all ran around parroting, "Who's happy?" And then we'd laugh.

(There is a knock on the door.)

PAUL: See. It's Nicholas. He's come after you.

(PAUL exits and a moment later enters with FATHER JAMES.)

SUSAN: Hello.

FATHER JAMES: *(To SUSAN)* Hello. *(To PAUL)* You've been to my church.

PAUL: Yes.

FATHER JAMES: *(To PAUL)* I need to talk to you.

PAUL: About what?

FATHER JAMES: Lori.

PAUL: Is she all right?

FATHER JAMES: We should have this talk in private.

SUSAN: *(To PAUL)* Do you want me to go?

PAUL: No, please stay. Father James, this is my sister, Susan.

FATHER JAMES: What's the game? You're playing with Lori's head, and I want to know why. You weren't lovers with her son.

PAUL: Is that idea so repellent to you?

FATHER JAMES: No. It's just that he wasn't gay. I know that for a fact.

SUSAN: *(To FATHER JAMES)* Father, I think you should leave.

FATHER JAMES: Are you in on this?

SUSAN: He'll stop seeing her. Trust me, he will.
It's best for both of them.

FATHER JAMES: Why that absurd lie?

PAUL: To comfort her. To make her feel better.

FATHER JAMES: It's driving her crazy.

PAUL: That's not what she tells me. She's happy
someone loved her son.

FATHER JAMES: What did you want with her?

PAUL: I wanted to see what she was like.

SUSAN: Paul, don't.

PAUL: Wanted to know what kind of home he came
from. At first I wanted to hate her.

FATHER JAMES: Why?

PAUL: Thought maybe that would make it easier for me.
But I couldn't.

SUSAN: *(To* PAUL*)* It's too late!

PAUL: *(Getting more and more manic)* I used to be a
good person. I used to be happy. I was. Tell him,
Susan. People liked me. Wanted to be around me.
My phone...it was always ringing. Always tons of
messages on the machine. Then one loss upon another
and another.

SUSAN: Paul!

PAUL: I thought I was strong. Be the perfect little
caregiver. I thought there was a light in me. That I was
blessed. I thought I could survive with love in my heart.
But that love has gotten eaten away with anger. Waves
and waves of it. And anger gets comfortable. But that's
not a way to live, is it? I needed to do something...do
something good. I remember good. I thought...bring her

comfort. That's your purpose now. Bring a fragment of relief to her day. Be of service to her. Maybe then... maybe then I would be granted a dreamless night. To be responsible for someone's lifelong suffering... Have you any idea what that's like?

FATHER JAMES: I don't know what you're talking about.

PAUL: *(Falling to his knees)* Bless me, Father, for I have sinned...

FATHER JAMES: This is not a confessional.

PAUL: My last confession was...years and years and years...

FATHER JAMES: Stop it!

SUSAN: Paul, no!

PAUL: I killed him! I watched his blood...

FATHER JAMES: Oh my God.

SUSAN: He was defending himself. The boy started it. Called him names...

FATHER JAMES: Called him names?!?

SUSAN: Hit him! Hit him first! Hit him hard! Then the boy fell. Hit his head. It was an accident. Self-defense. *(To PAUL, desperately)* Explain to him how it happened. Paul...explain it to him!

FATHER JAMES: If it was an accident, why didn't you tell the police?!?

PAUL: I was afraid. Do you want me to call them now? I will. Tell me what would be best for her. *(Getting up)* Should I go to the police? Should I confess to her?

FATHER JAMES: No! Not that! It would kill her.

PAUL: But why?!? Why is that?!?

FATHER JAMES: She'd blame herself even more.

PAUL: Why?!?

FATHER JAMES: God forgive me. You'll do as I say?

PAUL: Yes, I will. Whatever you say. Tell me! Tell me what to do!

SUSAN: Please...please, Father. Can't you just leave? It was an accident.

FATHER JAMES: You'll see her one more time... one last time.

PAUL: Yes.

FATHER JAMES: And you'll tell her...

(No one is paying attention to SUSAN. PAUL walks away from SUSAN and into LORI's kitchen. FATHER JAMES follows him, but stands at a distance from LORI and PAUL. LORI is seated. LORI does not hear or see FATHER JAMES. The following scene between PAUL, FATHER JAMES, and LORI has a dreamlike quality to it.)

PAUL: I wasn't totally honest with you.

FATHER JAMES: I believe...

PAUL: I believe...

LORI: *(Worried)* Yes?

FATHER JAMES: ...that I was probably your son's only experience.

PAUL: He was experimenting, I think. Young people do that. He might not have been gay.

LORI: It doesn't matter, does it?

PAUL: No.

FATHER JAMES: He said that if you knew about us...

PAUL: You'd probably laugh...

LORI: Laugh?

ACT TWO   63

FATHER JAMES: That it wouldn't be a problem.

LORI: No...it shouldn't be, should it?

PAUL: He said you were smart and loving...

FATHER JAMES: I envied him...

PAUL: ...being raised by you. He was lucky to have had you.

FATHER JAMES: He loved you...

PAUL: He loved you.

FATHER JAMES: I'm going to have to say goodbye. I have to get away from the city.

LORI: It's a sad city right now.

PAUL: Not from the city, but from the memory of Will. There's too much of him here.

LORI: You loved him that much?

PAUL: Yes. Yes, I did.

(PAUL *turns away from* LORI, *who is sitting quietly, and faces* DANIEL. *They are on the street.* PAUL *is in a raw emotional state.*)

DANIEL: Hello.

PAUL: I don't have any money.

DANIEL: Did you hear me asking for any?

PAUL: Sorry.

DANIEL: Don't you remember who I am? I'm Daniel. From A A.

PAUL: Yes.

DANIEL: You remember? That's good. How have you been?

PAUL: I really don't have time to talk. Sorry.

DANIEL: Give me a moment, please. I deserve it.

(PAUL *reaches into his pocket and hands* DANIEL *some change.*)

PAUL: Here, take this.

DANIEL: I don't want that. How dare you? (*Throws the change at* PAUL) I've never asked much of you. Only that you see me. That you look at me with some kindness. That you treat me nice. I'm not crazy. I'm your witness! I saw you kill the boy. I saw it all. I described you all wrong to the police. And they believed me. They did.

PAUL: Why?!? Why'd you do that?!?

DANIEL: Because I decided to love you.

PAUL: What do you want?

DANIEL: Nothing. I'm not asking for nothing. I love you.

PAUL: How could you love me? You don't even know me.

DANIEL: I know you better than you think. I know the dead boy haunts you. I know you follow the mother. I've been following you.

PAUL: Go to the police. Turn me in. I no longer care.

DANIEL: I'm not blackmailing you.

PAUL: Then what do you want?

DANIEL: You're lonely like I am. I understand you. And if you took the time, you'd understand me. We're both stuck. Stuck yearning for dead things. It's sad when it's only the dead you want to be with. All I want from you is a thank you.

PAUL: It would have been better if I had been caught.

DANIEL: That's not what I want to be thanked for.

PAUL: Then for what?

DANIEL: For my love. How many more times in your life will you be loved?

PAUL: Who are you?

DANIEL: I'm Daniel. A street person. Your witness. The man who loves you. We all need someone to love. And I chose you.

PAUL: But why?

DANIEL: Because you needed it. It just happened. Like those kids. That Romeo and Juliet. I saw the movie. That Leonardo kid and that beautiful girl. Didn't he just see her once and bam? I used to see you in the alley. And I'd wonder what is a handsome boy like you doing in a dark alley. If I were you, I'd be at parties and restaurants. I'd go to cool places. I'd get me a boyfriend. One to cuddle with at night. Once in the alley, I got so close to you that I could smell your skin. I loved the smell. The only problem with loving you is that you're white. I'm not very partial to white people. But God plays his jokes on all of us, doesn't He? This is nice... our talking like this.

PAUL: How'd you end up on the street?

DANIEL: *(Sarcastically)* As a baby, I always dreamed of it. It's a "spontaneous" kind of life.

PAUL: I'm sorry.

DANIEL: No, I am. It's just that nobody ever asked me before. Thank you. *(After a moment)* Things happen. A dead mother. A dead brother. An asshole stepfather. Lots and lots of pills. Wanting to disappear. Things happen. But once you move to the street, it's hard to get back. Every once in a while I try. But it hasn't worked yet. I imagine I have a couple of tries left in me.

PAUL: Try again. What would you like to do?

DANIEL: Be a movie star. Have Denzel's life.

PAUL: *(After a moment)* Would you like dinner?

DANIEL: Why yes.

PAUL: *(Reaching into his pocket)* Let me buy you dinner.

DANIEL: What do you mean? Give me money for dinner or take me to a restaurant?

PAUL: *(After a second)* Take you to a restaurant.

DANIEL: Really?

PAUL: Really. What kind of food would you like? Chinese, Thai, Italian, French...

DANIEL: A steak and fries...that's what I want...that's what I'd like.

PAUL: Daniel...I've stopped following the mother.

DANIEL: And you want me to stop following you.

PAUL: Yes. Please.

DANIEL: *(After a moment)* I will. Jesus, I feel sad right now.

PAUL: So do I.

DANIEL: At dinner...let's just talk about happy stuff.

PAUL: Whatever you say.

DANIEL: We'll tell stories from our lives. But only happy ones. The ones that make us laugh. And if we run out of them...

PAUL: I'm afraid we will.

DANIEL: Then we'll just sit there...quiet.

(End of scene)

Scene Twenty-seven

(Later)

(SUSAN and NICHOLAS are seated opposite each other.)

(LORI and FATHER JAMES are seated on a park bench.)

(PAUL and DANIEL are seated in two chairs opposite each other. They are in a restaurant.)

NICHOLAS: *(To SUSAN)* What with the promotion and the extra money...

SUSAN: *(Not listening)* What?

NICHOLAS: Susan, this promotion is a big deal.

SUSAN: I know.

LORI: I wonder what Florida will be like. My sister, she'll be company. You know those detectives? They don't get back to me so fast anymore.

DANIEL: That steak was real special. You should of had one. *(Looking around)* I wish I had nicer clothes. The waiter keeps looking at me.

PAUL: Fuck him.

DANIEL: You mean that?

PAUL: Yes.

DANIEL: *(Loud, laughing)* Fuck you!

LORI: That boy...that Paul. He's gone from my life.

FATHER JAMES: It's for the best.

LORI: You are always so sure...so sure of everything.

FATHER JAMES: No. Today, I did something I'm ashamed of. I forced somebody to lie.

LORI: Then why'd you do it?

FATHER JAMES: I wanted to relieve suffering.

LORI: You know how to do that? How grand.

FATHER JAMES: I want you...and people like that
Paul...to find some happiness...to feel safe again.

LORI: And you don't even know him.

NICHOLAS: You're tired. The baby is running you
ragged. Maybe we should get you some help.

SUSAN: No. I want to take care of my baby. I have to.
Nicholas, I'm afraid.

NICHOLAS: Of what?

SUSAN: I feel so alone.

NICHOLAS: But you're not. Tomorrow, we'll get a sitter.
Dress up, go to a trendy restaurant.

SUSAN: ...so dead inside.

PAUL: My sister and I...had one vacation when we
were kids. Only one. It was fun. Five days to be exact.
It was just before our parents were killed. Went to New
Mexico. We ended up in Questa...a one-street town.
It was surrounded by mountains. The Sangre de Cristo
Mountains. The blood of Christ. It was sunset. I thought
I was in a movie. Never saw anything like it. The
colors...the light. When I was a little boy and got scared,
I used to close my eyes and picture it.

LORI: Our sex...there was meaning to it, wasn't there?

FATHER JAMES: Yes.

LORI: And my son...he was a picture of beauty. I'll
dream forever what it would have been like to be a
grandmother. To be old and have my son irritating me.
To have grandchildren bored at my funeral. Or have a
gay son and his partner visiting me, taking me out. I'll
dream. These are the things I'll think about when I turn
out the lights.

NICHOLAS: At work today...John...you know who I'm talking about...said the most ridiculous thing...

SUSAN: Our baby...will never know his real uncle. The boy who took such good care of me for years and years.

NICHOLAS: Please, let me tell you about John...

DANIEL: I used to love the movies. My brother knew that. And whenever he had money...he'd take me. He'd take me to movies I liked. And he'd never make fun of me. They'd be old musicals...comedies with Doris Day. Shit like that. God, I loved those old movies. My brother never got it. But it was his gift. His gift to me. He'd buy me popcorn. Raisinets. He'd yawn during the movie. Sometimes sleep. But he never criticized them. "Wasn't that great?" That's all he would ever say. "Wasn't that great?" Have I ever been so generous? Have you?

LORI: It's a limited love you have for me.

FATHER JAMES: But it's love. I'll think about you. For the rest of my life.

LORI: I can't talk anymore. Let's just sit here until it's time for me to leave.

(NICHOLAS *is crying.*)

SUSAN: I'm sorry.

NICHOLAS: Don't say anything more. Not now. Please.

PAUL: I haven't thought about Questa in years. I wonder if it's still the same. Probably not. But I remember it being peaceful. Maybe I should go there. I told the mother I was leaving the city. I'll go there. I can't afford my apartment. I'll take what little money I have and go there. I have nothing here but my sister. And I have to let go of her before I ruin her life too.

NICHOLAS: I just want to sit here quiet. Happy to be with you.

PAUL: I'm going to that town in New Mexico.

DANIEL: To do what?

PAUL: To find if there's any good left in me.

DANIEL: You're looking to be invisible.

PAUL: Is that bad?

DANIEL: It's sounding like the streets.

PAUL: Maybe. Maybe not.

DANIEL: Don't be enamored with the streets.

PAUL: It might not be the streets. Couldn't it be a beginning?

DANIEL: Quiet. Let's just sit here. Don't you remember what I said? If we didn't have a happy story, then we would just sit here and be quiet.

FATHER JAMES: Lori...

LORI: Sssssh.

SUSAN: Nicholas...

NICHOLAS: Not now.

PAUL: All right. Quiet.

END OF PLAY

www.ingramcontent.com/pod-product-compliance
Lightning Source LLC
Chambersburg PA
CBHW052214090426
42741CB00010B/2530